Four Seasons

Year of Our Awakening

ISBN 978-0-9763016-6-0

Published by Scrivana Press

Iowa City, Iowa and Eugene, Oregon

Four Seasons

Year of Our Awakening

A Collection of Poems by Steven Harris

With notes and memories from

Steve's father, James Harris

December 2009

Dedicated to Mary Oliver and her book,

What Do We Know, Poems and Prose Poems

I read these poems at the best time for me.

She showed me how to put feelings into a few words.

She helped me see that simple things can bring big meaning each day.

I hope I can write more and discover the way that I can share all I feel.

Poems are my favorite creation.

Steve's Preface after the First Season

I hope you like my poems. I find writing helps me understand how I feel. When I finish a poem, I feel glad I can share it with others. That makes me believe I can be close to you.

Some days my poems express how I try to get better. Actually, they help me to get better.

When you read them, you can hear what I would like to say. One day I will read them aloud for you.

Next I hope to write poems about people. I cannot talk but I listen to everyone around me. I wish to let others know what I think.

Please tell me how you feel about this book. I would like to know.

February 25, 2009

Harbin, China

Written after reading Charles Darwin's *On the Origin of Species,* and a second book about the controversies ever since:

Some people felt Darwin made humans less than before. They did not want to hear that humans are like other animals. But I believe this doesn't make us less. We are like other species yet far more intelligent. I think we have free choice. We can make our lives better by what we choose every day.

In my life, I see I make many choices even though I cannot crawl or talk. I have much freedom to become better and happier. I like what Darwin taught us about life and change.

Steven Harris

February 23, 2009

Acknowledgments

Many people have encouraged this poetry – we thank all of you. We are especially grateful to Su Liying and all our family. Lois Harris, Krasna Svoboda, Stan Brown, and Heidi Wilde provided many useful suggestions.

We have valued immensely our visits to the Institutes for Achievement of Human Potential in Philadelphia, Pennsylvania, where Steve's treatment led to greatly improved vision, learning to read, and eventually to writing poetry. Miki Nakayachi and Rumiko Doman have been wonderful advocates and guides.

We are also grateful to Niki Harris who designed the book cover and guided our publication on Lulu.com.

Steve with Mama at Longwan (May, 2009). The front cover photo is from October.

Contents

Introduction

Dare

This story
is not just my story
but about courage and caring
of our family.

For any human
must dare to try
more than he thinks possible.
This book offers hope.

How Poetry Came Into Our Lives

By Jim Harris

My wife Liying ran during college, she was champion at mid-distance running. She told me success depended upon pace and confidence. Much later we found those same qualities helped us live with a brain-injured child, and love him well.

Our Steve has always loved music. And all of us had long ago discovered that his home therapy was very boring, all day every day for weeks, months, and years. So we placed a keyboard at the bottom of the inclined floor. If he crawled down this wooden slide that dominates our home, and pushed his chest onto the flat floor, he could reach his fingers onto the keys. Music was the best reward for each success. Later, during those years when he (and we) felt even more bored, we played songs that had been programmed into the keyboard. Often the melodies would energize him. He would hasten down.

This boy would have listened to music all day. We didn't notice, until he began treatment at the Institutes for Achievement Potential, that he was hyper sensitive to sounds. We gradually realized many noises bothered him. He had to wear headphones when we ate in a restaurant, and even then he might start crying. We would need to take him outside. And yet he loved music. The Institutes advised that he could only listen for ten minutes, at most, each day. As with all such advice, we listened with fear that if we didn't comply we would hurt Steve's chances of getting better.

Yet we didn't count his own hand on the keyboard as music, or the tunes that urged him down the inclined floor.

Finally, due to Steve's persistence with music, his programmers at the Institutes suggested that he read about music, and that he learn to read and write it. Still, just ten minutes a day. Steve's mother has delegated to me these intellectual parts of his program. Yet the thought of writing music alarmed me. I remembered my music teacher in eighth grade, I can picture his face and his long fingers writing notes on the blackboard. I had escaped from music study the day that summer vacation began.

One of the best things about Steve is that he forces us to learn and do what we never would have dreamed, or wanted to try. When the bookstore clerk showed me the obscure shelf with books about music theory, I picked *The Everything Music Reading Book*, right next to the Dummy's Guide. Later I returned to the same store and also took *The Everything Music Theory Book*.

I travel from Wisconsin to China where Steve lives as part of my job. I work on the conservation of cranes and wetlands, and have done so for 25 years. The place on Earth with the most crane species, and the most threatened crane species, is the Amur/Heilongjiang Basin in the border regions of China and Russia. Steve and his mother Liying live close beside one of the main tributaries to the Heilongjiang, the Songhuajiang, within a flyway for six species of cranes.

Each time before I leave Wisconsin for China, I gather a suitcase full of books, fifteen or twenty or more, to carry to Steve. Few English books are available in Harbin. This trip with the music books, however, was particularly long, across four continents. I traveled to China via habitats of Grey Crowned Cranes, Blue Cranes, and Wattled Cranes — passing through London, Nairobi, Kampala, Johannesburg, and Dubai before reaching Beijing.

Steve devours books. He loves them (he is a boy who loves much!), and like many brain-injured children who have the opportunity, he is a speed reader. He does naturally what speed-reading classes try to teach adults. He doesn't read words but sees the whole page at a glance and comprehends at least as much as I do. I like to read the same books he is reading, but what he completes during a few minutes each evening takes me many hours. I get a head start before my trips to China, and then catch up with him on additional books each visit.

Frankly I did not want to read these music books but Steve was impatient, and I faced necessity, for I would have to facilitate his writing of music. The reading music book seemed remotely familiar, the theory book less so. I found a place on the internet where I could download blank sheet music, and made a music communication card much like the card Steve already has for regular communication (a card that has all the letters of the alphabet plus punctuation and a few key words like "yes," "no," and "more;" by pointing to the letters one by one, he spells out what he is thinking) and his math communication card (that keeps growing as he moves into advanced math). This music card, however, was very simple . . . notes, pitch, clefs, rests, those numbers at the beginning that indicate the timing. We started with just one note at a time. No chords for us. He pointed, I scribbled down, and later copied everything onto the sheet music.

On November 21, 2008 he wrote his first piece. Then we played it on the keyboard. He already knew how to go from written music to music played. It was eight measures long, and quite pretty. We did this in the evening, because that is our only quiet time not filled with physical and breathing programs, massage, sensory stimulation, and so on. Steve was happy going to bed that night.

The next evening, he wrote another piece, with many more notes but because they were eighth notes, it too was eight measures long. After Steve played this piece he was so excited he could not go to sleep for hours.

I believe one of the reasons Steve has become a poet is that I get so sleepy in the evenings it is painful to stay awake. One evening later, I could not imagine another late night of happy, excited, wide awake Steve. I did not want him writing another piece of music just then. So I suggested he write a poem.

Poems are about feelings. Writing a poem was different for Steve, and for me, because of what we both remembered.

I remember a toddler who had just learned to walk. He loved people and eating but would not wear a hat. He always pulled it off his head. Threw it on the floor. One day, as I carried him on my shoulders, he waved his arms and hands up in the air. He laughed, the clouds were dropping rain. Rain became our game.

On March 10, 1997, I was called home to Wisconsin from a village in southwest China. I went straight from the airport to the hospital on March 13. Steve lay in a coma with wires coming out everywhere including the top of his head. Liying sat beside him, looking serene and confident. I will never forget. She was calling him back. That evening, as I spoke to him his face stirred.

The next day, he did waken.

Since Steve could not tell us, and no one else had been with the babysitter in her house but Steve and her own baby, we can only know what happened from the medical evidence and what the babysitter said and did not say. If she hadn't had friends over that morning, laughing and chattering, he probably would have napped, and been okay. But he had no nap, he spat out his macaroni and cheese at lunch, and after that he fussed and screamed so she could not watch her soap opera.

When her older son came home from school she sent him to fetch a neighbor who happened to be home and happened to be an emergency respiratory technician. He found Steve on the floor, hardly breathing. "Call an ambulance!" he cried.

Steve had become a shaken baby. The babysitter must have lost her temper, shaken him violently until she noticed that he no longer responded, then let him lie until her older boy came home. In the following days, the ICU doctor told Liying that Steve might live.

After awakening, during those early times, Steve would move his arms and legs without purpose, sometimes so much that he could not sleep at night. Liying and I took turns in the hospital in the dark hours, I remember the night nurses finally taking Steve so I could rest.

Liying found that if she dipped a sponge toothbrush in grapefruit juice, Steve would suck on the juice, his first purposeful response. But after he had a swallow test, doctors told us it was not safe for Steve to take liquids, they might slip into his lungs. Instead we had to pour liquid through a tube that reached down his nose and into his stomach. Before we left the first hospital, Terry one of the nurses kissed Steve on the neck. He smiled. I feel still grateful.

The pediatric rehabilitation doctor had told us that coming home from the hospital would be like bringing home our newborn baby. A second time.

The house was the same, just 14 months older, but Steve's books and toys, a red shirt and blue ball and diaper lay just where Mama had left them. Holding Steve, his first minute home, I felt the house big and empty and motionless. The time ahead pressed upon us, endless. I looked to Liying, we stood silently together, and felt the loneliness with our new child. Suddenly blankets rustled as Liying's mother Yu Lanfen was settling into the couch and reaching out for Steve. She had flown over from China and would spend the next five years with and beside him. If she hadn't had visa delays, we never would have known that babysitter.

They said we needed to be patient. With a brain-injured child, the answers come slowly. The child doesn't wake from his coma, sit up, and call, "Daddy." The return to life is gradual . . . weeks, months. Only as time passes do outlines of the life ahead appear. Yet lives of other children tell that most of the gains happen in the first three to six months.

We waited and hoped. But we felt those days so urgently, our hearts raced like sprinters.

I remember carrying him to the couch against the windows at the front of the room. I carried him like an over-sized newborn, my hand behind his neck to keep his head steady. During the earliest days, he had shown no sign of vision, no response when our faces came near or we waved our hand before his eyes. Yet now, as I leaned back against the couch so that Steve's chest lay against mine, his eyes turned toward the windows. He lifted his neck, raised his head inches and his eyes reflected the shine of afternoon sun on the cars sliding past along Highway 33, red or blue or white and bright flashes off the chrome. At those moments, Steve looked happy.

Steve did show improvements. He could hold his head up. His right hand groped for the toys that Grandma held brushing his fingers.

Yet so soon, it was the second summer. Never give up. Grandma and I took him every day to the park and put him in the toddler swing, with blankets stuffed all around to keep him stable and keep his head from scraping against the chains. Steve loved the motion, laughing and laughing. After he was three, he started going to a special classroom at school. Once a year, we would meet with all his therapists, with the teacher and aide for Steve, and school officials — surely, so many people gathered meant there would be progress — and write down how Steve was doing and what he should do next. I remember telling them, maybe when he was six, that Steve knew when we praised him for doing good work. He would smile proudly. Because he was legally blind, he received vision services. I remember the vision specialist using a light box and showing Steve silhouettes of the heads of the other children in the class. She noticed that he looked most at the silhouette of Neil, the Down's syndrome boy who often talked with Steve.

Liying was courageous, some might call stubborn. She believed we could still get Steve back. She took him to China — Liying had come to America from China in 1989 — where they tried Chinese traditional treatment for three months. Liying finally decided the doctor knew nothing that would help.

In 2001, a Russian friend arranged for a woman to come and live in our home and treat Steve with a method the Russians had developed for cosmonauts who stayed in space so long they lost their muscle tone. They needed to retrain their bodies. Lyudmilla brought a modified, miniature cosmonaut suit with hooks and rubber straps all over the outside. To our surprise, Lyudmilla was a pediatric rehabilitation physician and ran the lead rehabilitation clinic for her province. For six weeks, we had her all to our Steve. When Liying went away for a meeting in Washington, Lyudmilla, Grandma and I worked with Steve, each of us speaking a different language. It did not matter to Steve, or to us.

After Lyudmilla left, Liying took Steve to Moscow for treatment, a total of five times in the years that followed. I went with them once. We stayed in a hotel that had Chinese students living on the upper floors. Liying had stayed there before. It was October with that thin, rich light. Liying took us to the local outdoor market. She knew where all the best foods were, and the Russians knew her too and gave her good pieces. Steve loved the blue sky, frosty air on his face.

At the clinic, the doctor administering the electroencephalogram (EEC) had done that for all her career — Russian doctors rely on the EEC graphs of brain activity because few people can afford MRIs or cat scans. Highly skilled doctors work with EECs. Placing those graphs before us, she showed us how Steve's brain was starting to have alpha rhythms.

During the last of those trips to Moscow, Steve and Liying were taking the night flight from Beijing to Moscow. Seeing Steve, another passenger became excited, eager to tell Liying about his own brain-injured son. She wanted to sleep, but finally by the end of the flight realized that the story of this boy learning again to walk and talk was very interesting. Back in Beijing, Liying went to see the mother and son, and I later had the opportunity too. The family was following a treatment prescribed by the Institutes for the Achievement of Human Potential in Philadelphia.

In December of 2004, Liying went to the Institutes and took their course for parents of brain-injured children. She was very excited when she got home, wanting to turn our lives and schedules upside down with busy new activities. Her impatience was annoying. I felt tired from being alone with Steve for a week, but she had me sit with Steve and turn the pages of one of his picture books, the sort we had bought when Steve was fourteen months old and now still used for him. It had seemed to me that Steve liked these books but didn't really pay attention to them, looking off in different directions while I read aloud. This time she had me watch his eyes. With every new page, he turned his eyes for just a moment, a mere flicker across the page. "That's all he needs to see everything," said Liying. What impressed me was that he looked at every single page, and also that I never would have noticed if she hadn't told me to watch his eyes.

So our lives did turn upside down. We had a long wooden slide made, its inclined floor giving Steve a downward slope for learning how to crawl (we now have one slide in Wisconsin and another in Harbin). Much of his treatment related to breathing. Brain-injured children do not breathe well, and so the brain doesn't get enough oxygen; the brain works poorly without oxygen. Liying cut out all sorts of silhouettes in white and put them up against black cardboard on our walls to stimulate his vision. I went to the Institutes for parent training in April, then we took Steve. In May 2005, Liying and Steve went to live in her home city of Harbin where we could afford to hire four full-time workers to help Liying with his home treatment program seven days a week.

This period was difficult, I hated having them so far away. When we were together, the work with Steve was arduous. Every six months, we would bring Steve to the Institutes to have his treatment program assessed and revised. Once there was a magic afternoon at the Institutes, two hours while the therapist Miki evaluated Steve after another six months of our work at home. His vision had progressed enough so that Liying had been making white cards with black words written on them in letters 1.5 inches tall. Steve knew the words, eventually hundreds of words. He also knew words that Miki showed him, words we had never taught him. Then Miki showed pairs of words, and a third word (all new for him). Which of the first two words was like the third word? Steve promptly pointed to the correct one (two words were types of clothing, while the odd word was food; he pointed to the clothing). Moreover, Steve could follow her directions and gave the correct answer each time. I finally believed what Liying had been saying all along, Steve could understand everything we said.

Eventually, I realized he had understood everything for a long time. For example, he had heard us tell many people the details of what the babysitter had done, the criminal trial, and what we had felt, stories we never would have said in front of Steve had we known he was listening with full attention.

On another visit, Miki taught us "facilitated communication," a technique where we helped Steve to point out letters on a communication card. Actually, the first card was just "yes" and "no." Because Steve cannot hold the weight of his arm or wrist and still have enough control for pointing, and because he cannot separate his forefinger from the other fingers, we must hold his hand, and hold his finger out, lightly so he is free to move and point. Facilitated communication (FC) takes much learning by both the child and the parent. It is not easy. We progressed slowly. Since I had entertained Steve during boring parts of his program by imitating the voices of birds, and always saying the bird's name, we gained confidence with FC after I imitated bird songs and Steve spelled their names out. He knew all of them . . . blue-winged warbler . . . phoebe . . . black-capped chickadee . . . red-winged blackbird. Of my three children, he likes birds the most.

Steve's spelling has become quite good. He has a remarkable memory, and his vision improved steadily over the months. At first, we had needed to make our own books for Steve, with letters 1.5 inches tall, then 1.25 inches, then 1 inch. I would prepare the books on the computer and email them to Liying in China. Often they were stories from the family, about the skunk in the graveyard or the bear who stole our pancakes. I found the entire text of *Alice in Wonderland* on-line, arranged the book in three-quarter-inch letters, and emailed one chapter at a time. Eventually we could use big print books from the library. And finally he could read commercial books with regular type. He read fast and started reading adult books, too.

The Institutes asked that Steve write comments after each of the books he read. This request to write comments was good for Steve, but also the documentation of his reading could defend the parents if authorities questioned whether any home schooling was happening. I loved Steve's comments. By now, Liying and I probably knew our son better than almost any parents know their child, because we had been so involved in each tiny progress, such as drinking a full cup of water safely, steps that happen so naturally with regular children. Nevertheless, Steve's comments surprised us, at first simply by what he chose to write and later by his insight.

In the summer of 2007, I brought him *To Kill a Mockingbird*, forgetting that the main point of the story was a man trying to kill children, not a topic for a brain-injured survivor of assault. This threat was exactly what Steve wrote about:

> *I like To Kill a Mockingbird. I like Scout and Jem. Scary story about bad people. Children can be hurt. Boo saves Scout and Jem (and their dad Atticus).*

Steve's mind was moving ahead quickly during those years. He felt starved for experience, spending day after day in three rooms, getting outside only to be surrounded by dingy apartment towers in a Chinese city. He loved the travel to the Institutes, he loved sitting on the airplane, anything different.

Soon it was July of 2008. We were at summer camp in Inner Mongolia, at Keerqin Nature Reserve, the three days organized for children living on grassland threatened by years of drought where even the diminished herds now ate more than the land could sustain. Wildlife and rural people alike depend on finding a new balance linking water, people and this eastern edge of the steppe. The summer camp was one way we were helping the nature reserve build alliances and create common vision with the herdsmen. For the teaching, we used four languages — Mongolian, Chinese, Russian and American — since we had brought teachers from these diverse cultures together to give the children, and one another, a global sense of the challenges we face.

These July days brought a strong scent of hope, for the voices mingled our languages as the children ran from games to paints then stories of the grassland. The best rains in seven years had brought a million flowers of red and yellow and blue. My tasks had been to bring us together, teachers and students, and my wife and I had agreed to bring Steve out of the city to enjoy the result.

A brick path crossed the hillside of grass and flowers, sloping toward the lake before us, light blue of water against the green land. Beyond, grassland rose and faded into distant mountains purple and deep. We had pushed Steve and his wheelchair past the sheepskin yurts dyed festive colors, and now approached a long line of tables shaded by planks atop a metal framework. The children were crowded in the shade around the tables, water colors and papers shifting in the breeze, small hands catching them before they could fly.

Looking back, with the dome of the sky above and Keerqin grasses spreading below, larks singing in the air, Steve's joy is mingled with all the colors. "Let's take Steve on the horse," Liying exclaimed.

There was one horse, wearing bridle and Mongolian saddle and keeping to the shade of the dwarf oaks. No doubt he carried tourists from time to time. I had not been on a horse in 35 years, and suddenly felt overcome by a feeling I remembered well from years earlier, on the way to the dentist.

"How can we do this?" I asked, too nervous to think. We had talked other times about getting Steve on horseback, for it is a therapy often used for brain injured children. But I had thought we would go where someone knew what to do, like a horse therapist, with a corral enclosing us. Not on wild steppe and hillside.

"Do we walk beside him?" I asked, eying the wooden saddle so hard and threatening compared to our western leather or the soft English saddles.

Liying of course was right that walking beside would never work, Steve would fall off. She also insisted that I go up, she claimed she was not strong enough to hold Steve on top.

It was merely a delaying tactic, when I suggested we should ask Steve.

Of course Steve understood everything Liying and I said, and everything Liying said in Chinese too (I still had not learned Chinese). We didn't have the communication card with us but used my hand. He points left for yes, and right for no.

Steve pointed emphatically left.

I did not even get to sit in the saddle. Steve sat in the saddle and I sat behind. We went very slowly.

Looking at the photographs from that afternoon, we found Steve had his tongue out most of the time. It makes him look silly to other people, but he loves the breeze and feels it best on his tongue. I have my left arm reaching round and my hand spread across his chest, so he is upright and handsome and his face so alive. In so many other pictures, he slumps over, sitting in his wheelchair, for example. When we lined him up with the other children for the opening of the camp, the children all standing in rows with me and Steve at one end, he wears his black crane cap like the other children but slumps forward so that the brim hides his face.

One can't tell, from the way Steve holds his eyes, how much he is seeing and how much he is taking in the breeze and the song of larks or the Mongolian words around him. Steve is so quick to hear and remember. I found out later that the translating going from Mongolian to Chinese and back again made learning Mongolian words easy for him. That night he wrote on his communication card, "I loved feeling the horse. I could feel all his muscles moving under me."

I felt proud of Steve, upright and face shining. Yes, a little proud of myself too, after that ride on the pony. Even though my fears were foolish they were real fears nevertheless, I have fallen with Steve before.

In September 2008, he read T. H. White's *The Once and Future King,* one of my favorite books and very long. When he wrote his comments, he even picked one of my favorite parts, about the greylag geese. I liked how his thought jumped at the end, the logic seemed more like a poem than prose, so I asked him if I could turn his comment into a poem? *Yes.*

> *I wish that*
> *Arthur had kept his dream.*
> *Good people helped others.*
> *The king cared for all life in England.*
> *Because Arthur became other animals,*
> *he knew how they felt.*
>
> *I wish*
> *I could become a goose*
> *and fly to the North Sea.*

After I went back to America, I printed the poem and put it on my wall at work.

All this history rose around us as Steve and I sat on our bed on November 23, and I asked him to write a poem instead of music. We started by reading a few poems by Mary Oliver as inspiration. Then very soon, he began spelling out words on his FC card. I laughed, because his poem was about writing music.

Poetry likely arose, those ages ago, all mixed with music. And so it was for Steve.

Looking back, I am surprised we did not write more poetry in November. But his program kept us busy, and my time in China passed too quickly. We had been tasked with writing a book report for the Institutes, and from the books Steve had been reading he did not choose Stephen Hawking — as I expected — but Ross King's *Brunelleschi's Dome,* about the cathedral in fifteenth century Florence. Steve wrote:

> *Brunelleschi's dome took many years to build. At the beginning, he knew what he wanted to do but not how to do it. No one had built a dome as big as this one. He had to find a way to do what he dreamed.*
>
> *Brunelleschi did not want other people to know how he designed the dome, so he did not write down how he saw to make the dome. He did not use a wood frame that other people thought he should use. Instead he used circles of upright bricks to keep the dome tall. He knew he could succeed.*
>
> *Actually, I believe he wondered if he could make the dome tall, but he kept going on faith that he could.*
>
> *I believe that the achievements of Florence were possible because people believed they could do it. That is important for all people.*

At the end of that trip — the trip when I carried music books to China — I came back to America by way of Rome where I attended a meeting about migratory animals. I went to the Sistine Chapel, remembering the hours when Steve and I had also read Ross King's *Michelangelo and the Pope's Ceiling.* Looking up at Michelangelo's frescoes, I felt Steve. Then in Florence, I visited the dome and its cathedral Santa Maria del Fiore. Early my last morning, I climbed the 414 steps to the top of the campanile, to see the dome from up high and take pictures of dome and the heavens all around to bring home to Steve. The pictures show the sun glinting off the cross on the very top. I wrote a letter to him as I was traveling, and finished it as soon as I sat quiet in our Wisconsin house.

Reading the letter, I realized something was missing. I had not recognized what had been stirring between our two right hands and the communication card. Steve is ready to move ahead. I looked across the inclined floor, out the side windows of the living room at two burr oaks I have watched grow year by year. They are reaching too. Snow puffed up from each branch, each twig. I realized that Steve is already reaching for those sky places that many people do not know, or do not dare to go. He is already learning to use his inner voice, and that voice is a gift. Yes, we believe in talking, we believe urgently in walking, but he has discoveries already at his finger's tip that are important for all of us. . . what it is to waken from the dark sleep. That moment, our lives seemed not all about the future, or about our present hours sacrificed in stubborn, ceaseless run toward recovery. Looking out the window at oaks, I felt it is time to tell him that we will be writing from now on together, about this life, this awakening. We will be recreating in our own way this rise of trees, of spirit up toward our heavenly dome.

And yet, I still did not know that his poetry would be the path.

Winter

*Because I cannot talk,
I write my thoughts
and then I wait for you to
answer.*

Wrens Alive in My Heart

Music is my favorite.
Dare I write
music as it feels to me?

I feel so much when I hear music
I want to sing.
I wish I could sing like the birds!

When I imagine the song I would write
it is like the wrens alive in my heart!

November 23, 2008

Steve has trouble keeping his balance when sitting. To give him stability while using his communication card, I often sit behind him on our bed, with one leg on either side. After he wrote his musical pieces, I laid the keyboard across our legs. With my left hand, I held the sheet music so Steve could see, while my right hand supported the weight of his wrist and held his forefinger out. He moved his finger confidently to play the notes, one key at a time. In the same manner, with facilitated communication, he points to one letter on his communication card, then the next and next.

As he wrote this poem, he paused for me to scribble down each line. I felt increasingly surprised as the poem emerged, and called out to Liying in the other room.

My dim memory, of trying myself long ago to write a poem, involved struggle and many cross outs and long pauses when I could not think of another word much less a line. Steve did not write quickly but he never hesitated. After he was finished, I asked him for the title — he spelled it right away. I told him we would look at his poem again the next day, in case he wished to change anything. He did not change even a word.

34

Gifts for Me

I like gifts.
I believe gifts have changed everyone
even deadly enemies.
The best gifts are simple
like song.
Little gifts mean the most to me.
Yesterday
Daddy found I spoke Chinese!

January 23, 2009

In summer 2008, Steve was almost daily saying words that I could understand, and many more words I could not understand. At his September visit to the Institutes, he received a language victory because he could speak more than 25 English words, and more than two couplets — even though many of these words he said only once, because he has such trouble controlling his breathing. Steve was very proud of that victory.

But when I saw him in China in November, and again early this visit, he was not saying any words except, *No!* and once, *Jim*. I wondered why. The other night, taking him to dinner, he said, *Hao chi* — that means delicious. I asked him if he could smell good food (I cannot smell much of anything). He pointed, *yes*. I asked if he often spoke Chinese words, again he pointed *yes*.

Later he wrote that he mostly talks in Chinese. That is natural, because he is with Chinese speakers all the time. Since I have worried and wondered why his talking seemed to regress in November, I am happy to have this mystery solved.

Unfortunately, there are very few Chinese words I can recognize. For Steve, successful talking — just like success with facilitated communication (FC) — depends on both people. If others cannot hear, he is alone with his thoughts.

Leave Behind

I want to do more pawate
because I am getting strong.
I want to go
faster and farther
every time.
Some day
I will leave pawate behind.

January 25, 2009

Pawate (pronounced pa – wa – TEE) is Pinyin Chinese for the inclined floor, or slide. It is much easier for a child to crawl down a slide, because gravity helps. The challenge is to continue onto the flat floor.

Some lines of Steve's poems stay in my mind. So often, as he comes down pawate, I give back words from this poem, only I get the order reversed, *go farther and faster.*

Every Morning

Birds have beautiful voices.
I love the wren.
I hope to live near wrens,
to hear them every morning,
to feel the lift in my heart,
and share it with you!

January 27, 2009

Facilitated communication (FC) is a remarkable merging between us. It can easily happen, however, that I influence or change what Steve writes. When I don't pay attention, I find sometimes Steve writes a word I expect even if it doesn't make sense. Yet when I relax and empty myself, Steve's forefinger surprises me often . . . with almost every poem! Once he spelled out Santa Maria del Fiore. I had forgotten that was the name of the great church in Florence that held its dome into the sky.

As time passes, with the interplay of our fingers, Steve's own voice has been emerging. So long voiceless, Steve's thoughts have long turned back on themselves. He has learned much we do not know . . . from regaining sight, from a solitude no child would choose but Steve wears with grace. I realize that yes, I do influence his words, sometimes by mistake, and also like any parent does. Any child learns his language from mother and father. For any parent, it is a challenge to teach and nurture without controlling. Yet Steve listens out of a need and habit other children do not have . . . listening is his chance to learn what is happening to him, to prepare, his best way to survive.

And the opposite is also true, my words, my hopes are changed week by week as I listen to Steve.

Maybe this is my favorite of his poems so far. The lift at the end is much like a wren's song.

A few minutes after Steve wrote this poem, he became upset. When I got his communication card out, and changed positions for both of us so he could FC, he wrote, *I want to believe I will get better.*

Contradiction

Firecrackers are noisy
people like to make them explode.
I startle and jump.
I wish they would go away
but
I love the
bang, bang, bang.

January 28, 2009

Steve and I lived through Spring Festival — Chinese New Year — that
turned our "quiet" part of the city into a combat zone. Fireworks day and
night. They echoed off the tall buildings, like thunder in coldest January.
Our apartment complex authorized firecrackers but only in the courtyard
that happened to be right out our window. Steve loves sounds but is overly
sensitive and often startled by loud noises. Those guiding his treatment
would have been horrified that we often hurried to the window to see (and
of course, hear) all the more.

Dream of God

I like to see his God
what Michelangelo dreamed
high above us.
We find how the world began
and we learn how the world will end.
I am glad to live between
and know how man became.

I am really good
despite all I will never do.

February 2, 2009

In September, Steve and I had read *Michelangelo and the Pope's Ceiling*
about the making of the Sistine Chapel frescoes, then in November
Brunelleschi's Dome about the cathedral in Florence – both set in
Renaissance Italy. These books are by Ross King. That place and period is
perhaps my favorite, and I was delighted that Steve liked both books.

He wrote a poem about Michelangelo. After reading this poem often, I
found my memory of the Sistine Chapel and my recent visit had changed
– as if Steve had sat beside me on the bench around the outer wall, when I
craned my neck to look high above.

Colors in My Mind

Cold outside
the studio felt hot
so many colors all over the room!
So many landscapes against each wall.
Look!
Each one has different colors
different feelings.
One has coarse brown and red all across
ready for more paint.
My uncle said I should paint too!

February 2, 2009

Every evening we look in the fat volume called *Art Treasure a Day*. Each day of the year has a painting and a quotation. October 6 was van Gogh's A Starry Night, one of my very favorite paintings. Steve wrote, *I like how van Gogh shows the stars as they feel to us.* I remember a year ago when my mother and Steve and I went out to see the meteor shower. We did not see it, but Steve did see stars. Not so long before, his eyes could not.

During Chinese Spring Festival, I asked Liying's cousin if we could visit his studio – he is a successful landscape painter, one of the best known in Heilongjiang. Another cousin offered to take us, and on the way go by the snow sculptures for which Harbin is famous. Steve had absolutely no interest in the sculptures, though we wheeled his chair through bitter cold air for most of an hour. Both cousins expected the stop at the nearby art studio to be a brief in-and-out, a chance to get warm.

Walking out of the cold, my glasses fogged up and a blur of bright colors swept all around us. Steve came alive. He had questions. *How do you paint? What will you paint next? How do you feel?* Later, I asked him what poem was his favorite of this Spring Festival Period . . . *Colors in my mind.*

40

Going Outside!

I like to go outside
I like getting my coat and boots
I like bumping down the stairs
I like when I feel the cold on my face
I like the sun in my eyes
I like the sky so tall and blue
I hope one day
never to go back
inside.
I will crawl away!

February 6, 2009

Many days, Steve tells me his favorite moment is the outside time. Winter in Harbin is fierce. Even though we have a wide courtyard below us, we have to time our foray to catch the sun.

Going outside can be very tiring for the two adults who take him, because Steve is getting bigger, more and more erratic about standing and bearing his own weight. Often he raises both feet into the air, it must be fun to swing with the breeze in your face.

Liying has more patience than I, helping him balance and move one leg forward then another. Liying carries such serenity and confidence in Steve and his future, she is good for both of us.

41

Just Once!

Sometimes I wish
I could have my Daddy
beside me every day.
I miss him when he goes away.

I wish we could read every night,
I wish we could laugh and go outside,
I wish we could write poems.
Just once I wish he could stay forever.

February 8, 2009

For my work, I am often leaving Harbin on short trips. Steve doesn't like
it. I feel terrible, too, and now the poetry makes it harder to leave. He has
such beautiful things to say, gifts for me.

He cannot communicate more than yes or no, or short phrases, with
anyone else on his communication card. The workers can't even get to yes
or no. For Liying, English is still awkward, not intuitive after all these years.
Also, Steve can be sloppy in pointing to letters. For him, a third inch off to
either side is no big deal but any letter could be one of eight neighbors.
Liying gets discouraged, Steve gets emphatic and then stops trying. Liying
tried making a communication card for Chinese, but the characters are too
many and too diverse. Steve reads Chinese, and understands everything
spoken around him but cannot write.

Believe

Foretelling the future —
do you know what will happen?
I believe Mary knows!
She watches me,
she hopes I will move faster and farther,
she will help me believe.
If I believe
my dream will come true.

February 14, 2009

Last night I brought Steve the envelope from Marina in Russia, with an icon inside. A boy who cannot move around or pick up things does not have possessions, or need or use them in the way the rest of us do. Steve is, however, learning to pick up books if they are not too big and if they are close beside him. But he immediately puts them in his mouth – so I must hold onto them too, at a slight distance from his face.

I feel the many things I bring him are gifts in the sense that birds are for you or me, they fly within our sight, and we enjoy them, and then they fly away. Steve loves the books and remembers them well, but doesn't look back to the physical objects. He is content when I suggest we might give one to someone else to enjoy. He doesn't "own" things.

So I haven't felt that he receives gifts in the way of other children.

But when he reached his hand into the envelope last night, he chortled. He doesn't do this often, he was just like a boy opening a present! I stopped and asked him if he knew what was inside. *Yes.*

Did you hear Mama and me talking about it this morning? *Yes.*

He was so happy and smiling when he (we together) pulled the icon out of the envelope.

Courage

My wish is to have a life
like any boy,
just to carry my share
of fun and work,
sleeping in my own bed
that does not move
and squeeze the breath out,
waking to do what I want,
even nothing.

I hope I can find the courage
to become a normal boy.
And then I will tell you
how it feels!

February 23, 2009

Today was again tiring and hard for him on pawate, and I pushed. My expectations stir up doubt and make him angry when I remind him that he is strong enough to come down that incline each and every time.

Just now he wrote, *Courage.* I admire this boy!

Every night, before "bedtime," we strap him into a vest with seven loops that hook onto a breathing machine. The machine runs from a compressor on the back porch, connected by a wire through holes in the wall into the kitchen and through the kitchen and another wall into our bedroom. Even with the compressor itself far away, we listen to the breathing and creaking of the machine all night.

His is not really a bed, just blankets on the floor. Safer that way, he cannot fall off. To make it easy for us to tend to the machine, we all sleep on the floor. As for Steve, he must stay in the same position on his belly all night, and have the straps contract around his chest every second and third beat, to exhale deeply.

When he wakes in the morning (often we wake him up), it is off to the races again, hurrying through the entire program to stay on time . . . then finally, get back into the machine next night.

We accept all this. When we began four years ago, Steve was legally blind. We had never heard him speak any words, except (for me at least) in a recurring joyful dream.

A Special Thing

Help for me is a very special thing,
many times I cannot do what I mean.
My arm doesn't push,
my deep thought doesn't reach my leg,
sometimes I cannot do what any of us want.
At moments like these
I need you to believe in me,
I need you to give me confidence
and tell me you believe too.

But I know another day
we'll have another chance.
You are my Daddy and I love you.

February 24, 2009

Today was another tough day. My time would soon be over, I had to return to America for two months. This departure was much worse than going the short distance from Harbin to Russia, or to Inner Mongolia. Worse, we had to prepare videos of Steve's program and progress, especially pawate. The activities had to be in the right order. We wanted the Institutes to see what was really happening for Steve, so they could send us advice by email. But we also wanted to show Steve at his best.

With Liying behind the camera and the tape rolling, Steve would lie smiling but not moving on the incline. Or, right under the camera, he would put his head down on his arms to rest. I am on the floor too. Like Steve, I am sick of doing this pawate for four years, and I believe he can come down fast on the incline when he wishes. I kept my tone good for the video, but I was getting angry, and Steve hears like an owl.

This evening, writing down the lines of his poem, I felt the thrill that something had changed, a reality different from what I thought — Steve is not choosing to loiter on the incline. Without excitement or joy, without energy flowing through him, he can only use deep thought. Yet deep thought doesn't move the legs. I felt scolded and beautifully forgiven all at once.

I asked Steve why he sometimes bites himself, coming down the slide. He replied, *I bite myself because I cannot move my leg or arm. Biting helps me move.*

Spring

*I have learned to find what is
best for me
and hold it deep.*

To My Friends

How are you?
I heard you got poisoned
when you helped the trees.

People did not believe you at first,
you had to go to Beijing.
What did you feel on the hospital bed?
Did you lose hope that you can help the world?

Stay brave, stay confident!
What you do makes all the difference for me, for trees, for
you!
You have beautiful art
and beautiful lives.

I hope you love all that you have dared to do.

May 3, 2009

I was in America when Liying heard on the national Chinese news that
the children had been poisoned. They were the students Steve had
known from last year's summer camp, including the girl Steve had been
exchanging letters with for a year. The students had volunteered to help
the nature reserve spread a liquid on the trunks of elms attacked by
beetles. In dry years, the beetles eat all the leaves; if that happens too
often, the trees die.

The students had worked in the morning, and by afternoon some felt sick.
The local doctors told children and parents nothing was wrong. Finally
parents brought their children to Beijing — most children had never been
there before — where the hospital discovered chemicals in the children's
blood. They stayed for treatment, as many as 600 children, parents,
teachers and nature reserve staff waiting in Beijing. All children recovered.

When I came back to Harbin, I asked Steve if he wanted to write to them.

After the Sun Goes

For me, time is short,
the chance to sit outside with you,
the evening warm and wind in our faces.

The children stand near,
they want to see what I write.
I love to have children around and talking.

In my dream, we are
always like this,
between day and night,
with our lives waiting
to give us this moment of happiness.

May 6, 2009

We feel so happy about the warm weather. Every day we go outside,
usually late afternoon when his physical program is done. Children and
families are eager to emerge after the long winter. I bring out books, the
communication card, paper for writing.

I ask Steve what he would like to do, choices. Often he will spell *p o e m*
on his card. On other days, I will ask him if he would like to write a poem,
or I even suggest a topic. He has no idea of the theme until we sit with the
communication card. He pauses no more than a minute, then starts writing
with the entire poem in his head.

I am curious about how and when he composes, and so I often ask him.
While many poems come while he is working with breathing or patterning
or pawatee — he saves them until we sit quiet together — this time he
writes in the very moment, as we sit on a bench and the sky softens above
us.

Because I Remember

Because I was blind
seeing is special to me.

Because I can remember
when my eyes
could not find any flowers,
I love each time
we meet them.
I love each bird
that flies before us,
each tree that
runs up to the sky,
I love the blue.

Each day I love your face
the wrinkles I can see now,
the affection you have
when you see me.

May 9, 2009

We sit on the bed, shortly before sleep time. I feel excited inside as each
poem begins, yet it is also the hardest moment because most evenings
I have no idea what he will write. Poetry is so unexpected that I always
worry I will not understand him.

This poem brought tears. Here is my son telling me what he sees with such
gratitude. I remember the early days after the coma, as Steve lay on his
back and moved his limbs randomly. No vision at all. I remember thinking
I would not mind, I would be content even if my son could not see, I would
tell him about colors and birds and sky.

Pause

Because days are short
I like to stop and feel what we have done
glad to read poems and
dream about what I would write,
and then to write
exactly that.
And find that holding my breath
helps me to see more.

When we pause like this,
I feel most close to you.

May 13, 2009

He has never liked when we read aloud to him. He reads incredibly quickly, and we are too slow. But with poetry he has learned that the sounds of words, our voices, do matter. Poetry is music.

When he finishes his poem, I read it aloud. He gives me the title. Then I read it once more and ask if he wants to make changes. He doesn't. Twice I have suggested changing a single word, both times due to rhythm. But both the next mornings, speaking the poems in my head, I knew his original words had been better. We changed back.

Counting Blessings

How can I give thanks for this life?
I can see the sun
the sky
blue or gray or black with stars,
the light different every evening.

I hear children.
They play
even though the sun has gone,
running far and fast is easy for them.
They talk,
they laugh
as if each moment would last forever.

I sit, I listen
I make some words on paper.
I live my own life.
I give thanks.

May 19, 2009

Steve has extraordinarily acute hearing – regularly, the sounds are too much for him and he has to wear headphones to reduce noise. It is hard for him to be in a room full of people.

Months ago, I had wanted to give Steve the ammonite fossil I brought from Africa, cut in half with the inside polished. I also wanted to show him the fossil sand dollar. I left Steve and went into the other bedroom, mentioned this quietly to Liying (not wanting to let Steve know what I was about to do) and was surprised that she had already shown one of the fossils to Steve that day – which one, I whispered!? We fumbled about a bit, murmuring past each other with clumsy English, until I figured out he had already seen the sand dollar.

When I went back into Steve's room, he was laughing, very pleased, and laughing more. I asked him if he had heard Mama and me talking. *Yes.* Was that why he laughed? *Yes. Mama already showed me the sand dollar . . . today, when I woke up.*

I asked Steve if he knew what an ammonite was. *An ancient animal that lived in the sea.* Liying doesn't know the name of either ammonite or sand dollar.

Daring to Sit

Happiness comes in small pieces,
I never know
when or how I will feel happy.
I wait.
I hope.

Suddenly it comes
like wind in my face
or sun through clouds,
right before me
the world looks new and
very pretty
very full and never the same.

Any evening may be the time
I see just the perfect flower
or have rain touch my cheek.
I wish you will sit with me.
We will see what happens.

May 20, 2009

We wrote in the courtyard after dinner. No sun this time, the sky looked like
rain and once I felt a big drop. Steve later told me he added the line about
rain at that moment. He says he sometimes thinks about poems during
the day. I assume he must start with words and lines. Does he always put
them together into poems?

At the Top

Going up the stairs
we work hard
we breath, we feel
how high we have come.
When we stop to look,
the lake is far below.

The birds sing in the trees,
we see the sun through leaves new green.
We hope to go higher
than the birds, trees
higher than the sun.

We always hope like this
but today it may happen
beyond the top of the stairs.
Even now, we are close
we are ready to climb
the rest of the way.

May 22, 2009

We spend so much time indoors, in that small apartment, we are all excited when we go on trips. Liying has arranged for us to visit Longwan in Jilin Province, lakes among mountains not far from the border with North Korea. These lakes formed in craters of ancient volcanoes. The morning after we arrived, we walk down to one lakeside and take a boat ride. Back on land, we look up the mountain so steep there is not a trail, only a stairway rising among the trees. Before Liying can lead us away, I ask Steve if he wants to go up.

The student and I carry him the long distance to the first landing above the lake. Grateful to sit on the bench, we pause for Steve to write. Before that moment, none of us (except maybe Steve) has decided to go higher. Liying is against it, "We are only a third the way up! Too high!" My legs already feel very tired, and I wonder if the way down will be difficult on legs and balance.

Rising Over Water

Because I cannot walk
two men came with us for our journey,
carrying me up and down.
We crossed the stream many times
each climb scared me when we went up the stairs.
I was glad when we reached the waterfalls
and I got out with Daddy and Mama.

We stood beside the water.
We heard only the great fall of the stream,
and I did not mind
all that fear
or the bumps that made me ache.
Waterfalls are splendid.

After we came back
to warm rooms and my bed
I found a beautiful memory
of struggling over bridges
and what life is like when you leave
normal feelings behind.
I am so tired.
I am so glad

we left roads to follow that stream.
Day is far gone,
I will sleep.

May 22, 2009

We went back to the hotel for lunch, then set out again. Typically, since I alone don't understand Chinese, I had no idea of our afternoon plans.

Eventually Steve got so upset with the bumping and aching that he refused to ride any farther in the wheelchair. I took turns carrying him with the stronger of the two men, or with the student. We were all exhausted.

This poem was the end of Steve's day. He went right to bed.

Waiting by the Lake

Sitting by the lake,
I am looking for some secret hope
that today will show us
how God reaches down to Earth.
Can he stretch his arm from the cloud?

I believe it happens another way
the wind,
or bird song from the mountain
or his voice inside my heart.

May 23, 2009

I had never planned a religious education for Steve. He discovered it, in the books I gave him to read. Of course, Santa Maria del Fiore and the Sistine Chapel mean little without God. Then Steve wrote his comments in summer 2008 about *The Secret Life of Bees.* That novel is so full of courage and suspense, racism and guilt (young Lily thought she had killed her mother), that I had hardly noticed what Steve chose instead to write about, the Black Madonna in the livingroom: *Lily learns that friends help her and Mary watches over her. I hope Mary may watch me too. Mary can help me work and believe that I can walk.*

These comments led to other books, and to Steve "talking" with me about faith and forgiveness (as when he wrote, *I am really good despite all I will never do).*

Each Minute

Back at home,
we remember
a far away mountain,
kept beautiful by spring.

The trees were fresh green,
this their short promise
that life can be lovely
and we perfect.

So many moments become
a single feeling
now that we are looking back.

May 24, 2009

Steve wrote this poem just a short time after we returned home from
Longwan. Oddly, when we sat on the bed and I asked what he wanted to
do, he told via FC that he wanted to teach me how to write poetry. I asked
him how. He replied, *I will write a poem.*

The Institutes staff has told us not to be testing our children, we should
not act as if we don't believe they can read, or understand, or think. Lack of
trust discourages. Yet I am so surprised by each poem, by how he thinks
them, how quickly, I keep asking again and again, as if I am trying to touch
a face I thought I would never see again.

His mind holds me still. He studies calculus at age thirteen, but he can't
show his work so he does the problems in his head, points to the answers
digit by digit on his math card, almost always correct.

He is not just any boy. I look to him to discover myself.

Summer

We sit among strangers
like us,
we do not talk to anyone.

You do not speak Chinese,
I do not have breath for words.
It is lonely,
no chance for conversation.
Yet I love the evening . . .

Poetry Warms My Heart

Today I can write again.
I have much to tell you.

In this time,
I have tried to work hard
but the legs do not answer my best thoughts,
my arms are weak and do not push.
I have hoped I could find a way to succeed.

Now I can tell you
how sorry I am not to move.
Let us pray together that
we feel differently,
that poetry warms my heart.

June 30, 2009

Steve wrote this poem the morning after I arrived back in Harbin. The first chance we had to sit together, he wanted to write.

It is a very long time – scenes from Shakespeare? – since people talked in poetry. Yet that is what Steve has just done. Whenever I return, his first poem or two feels like conversation, catching me up on the important news inside him.

66

Reaching

Tadpoles do not have legs.
They must jerk their whole bodies.
I try to move the same way,
wriggling and rocking.

I want my arms and legs
to get strong.
Then I can push,
then I can crawl.

I see my hands reaching across the floor.
My fingers ripple over the keyboard.
They look so alive,
like my hopes.

July 7, 2009

Since I am beside him on the flat when he comes off pawatee, I too see his hands reaching across the floor, and his fingers have rippled today over the keyboard that I took out of its box. He loved having the music again. Earlier in the day, Steve read all his poems from May in order. Then I asked him to choose the best ones. He selected ten, all of them poems I like a lot. He "missed" only one of my favorites. I had done this partly to make him think about what he liked in his poetry. He has read enough of others' poems to have a good ear.

I have thought that he may not find fresh topics after writing so many poems during the same, very limited routine that binds his days (he writes often about freedom!). I had suggested he write about his hands, but was expecting him to start with his fingers, and stay with hands all the way through. He has the confidence and fun to choose his own perspective on any topic – very special for a thirteen-year-old, or anyone.

In Longwan in May, Liying and I had found dark clouds of tadpoles in a shallow pool steeply downhill from the road. We climbed back to get Steve and carried him down for a look.

In Your Hands

Long ago when I was
small and injured,
when I could hardly see
anything at all,
Grandma held me
day by day.
She made me feel warm,
she made me feel I was special.
I wanted to come out among people.

Whenever I see her,
I remember
how all my life
comes from her.

I have one secret to tell her:
I will never forget
caring hands
and your voice, Grandma.

July 7, 2009

This time when I got back from Russia, Grandma was staying with us to be
the fourth patterner (we need four people to do this sensory activity, called
patterning, where we move his arms and legs to a rhythm or sequence at
scattered times through the day). I was thinking about themes for Steve to
write about, and wondered what if anything he remembered from the five
years Grandma spent with him in America. I wouldn't have been surprised
if he had remembered nothing, he was only six when she left and still a
very injured boy. But he told me he did remember, so I suggested he write
about Grandma back then. He had already written another poem today,
responding to my suggestion that he write about his own hands.

With Thoughts Inside

Sometimes four boys play,
sometimes more,
they run and shout.
I wonder what I would be like
if I could call to others
loud and quick
like them.
Would my heart be different?

I do not think so
but I believe
my spirit has grown strong
because I must hold my thoughts inside
where I have time
to think and think again.

Could I be different with a different body?
I will never know.

July 9, 2009

Like most cool evenings in summer, the courtyard is noisy with people including lots of running children. Steve went down first with Geng and Guo, they sat on the bench for his water and snack (Geng, Guo and Mei work full-time with Steve). By the time I arrived for the poem, Steve had been watching the children for twenty minutes.

I am so used to Steve that I missed an irony in his poem. His mind is brilliant, although his body holds him silent and still. Yet the injury was to his brain, not his body.

Rainbow

Lying on my bed
I see the sky out my window
the clouds change
all the time,
today had blue and gray and white.

The rain came hard
while the sun shone,
I could hear the water
in a thousand drops
hit the ground
and bounce.

I could smell fresh moisture;
but from my bed, I could not see the rainbow
across the east sky.
Daddy carried me that way, for my first beginning wish
that I will never forget
how surprising is the world.

July 9, 2009

Yesterday, I suggested to Steve that he write about the sky and clouds he
could see when lying in his bed. I notice he often looks out the window,
and from that angle only the sky is visible. Maybe he planned to write this
poem anyway this evening, but first we saw a full rainbow. We stood on
our porch and looked east away from the sun (rainbows always are away
from the sun). There was just a trace of a second rainbow above, Steve
could see that too.

Neither of us had ever seen a rainbow in the city.

Fly

Going down the stairs
I looked out the window,
I saw a swallow fly by,
made me think
what if I could fly?
How the world would look
rising and falling,
like breathing.

Each of us knows
the world in our own way.
But I can imagine and feel in
all those ways,
like the swallow and
the boy going down the stairs.

I am glad my mind can fly.

July 18, 2009

Steve wrote this first swallow poem while we sat in the courtyard in the
early evening.

As always, we had just carried him down the stairs, Geng in front carrying
his legs and me behind with the rest of Steve. He happened to look out the
window on the landing (half-way down) in that moment as we passed.

Old Man Learns with Children

He was an old man
but he decided to learn painting
with young children
who learned
faster than he did,
who felt more confident
than a famous man
who was afraid
he could not
paint monkeys
or bamboo.

He looked at the children painting.
He learned slowly but well.
By the end of the book,
he loved his art.

He showed us
we should always dare new actions
whatever age we are.

July 19, 2009

I asked Steve if he wanted to write comments or a poem about the book
Painting Chinese, A Lifelong Teacher Gains the Wisdom of Youth by
Herbert Kohl. Steve preferred writing a poem. He wrote the first stanza
early in the morning but we were interrupted. He finished in late afternoon.
This poem is a good summary of the book, but I wonder if the whimsy of
the first stanza was lost to the rest of the poem because of the interruption.

First Memory

Long before I could understand
what you said,
I remember the light at night.

I remember lying in the dark
on the floor
that was my bed
and looking up at shadows moving
against the light upon the ceiling
and feeling
so comfortable
that I would never wish to change that moment.

Daddy's voice came calling me.
Mama whispered.

July 20, 2009

Steve wrote a poem just after dinner. Because we could not go outside due to rain, we had more time in the evening after we finished all our regular activities. He opted to write this second poem.

I had suggested he write about his earliest memory.

Clouds

Because we believe that
new clouds grow every hour,
we watch the sky
whenever we can.
Even now the clouds
move fast.

I find their colors always change
as if the sky painted them.
Now I know the sun rules the heaven
it roves above the clouds,
it turns them
black or gray or
silver or pink or
pushes them aside to show the blue behind.

When I watch the clouds,
I feel my deepest hopes
and my spirit rises tall
as all towering storms
over our city.
The sky is my friend,
my inspiration.

July 22, 2009

We have had so much mixed sun and rain, with clouds rushing by and up,
that I suggested Steve write about the clouds. He watches them anyway,
whenever he can.

74

Dearly Care

Looking again at this land,
I remember last year,
the lake where we swam,
the mountains beyond
above them the clouds,
today gray,
that wind on my tongue.

Many days have passed
since we first knew Keerqin.
The grassland looks the same,
I have changed.

My eyes can see farther and deeper,
my thought has grown
so I wonder bigger questions
like why we gather on this ground,
what can we hope the sky will feel
because we humans talk different languages,
but we dearly care about an identical
future for this Earth.

July 24, 2009

He wrote the early lines in the men's yurt (tent) after lunch the first day of
summer camp at Keerqin in Inner Mongolia. Steve got half of the poem
down onto paper then we had to stop for Opening Ceremony and art that
Steve liked because he joined the other children. He finished late in the
day, sitting on the steps of the main building where we could see the lake
and blue mountains beyond.

Mulberries

We drove into mountains.
It is not blue here.
It is green and dry and hot,
we sat in the small shade of short bushes
hiding from the sun.

From below, the bushes
were rich and deep.
We see leaves dark,
shining,
Yanqiu finds mulberries
green and bumpy, some red,
they taste sour.

Even here in Inner Mongolia,
I find reminders of home,
our purple mulberries big and sweet.
But these in Keerqin are extra,
strange and familiar both.
I am always close to home.

July 25, 2009

This poem turned a hot, dusty morning into insight and a surprising descent not just one level but two levels down. We wrote only a short way into the second stanza when we had to leave for the lowlands. We did not complete the poem until late afternoon, after Steve did two pastel drawings of the lake and (again) blue mountains, although the second time we noticed the nearest were green. Steve was happy that he could do art. Our dear friend, art teacher Yanqiu was sitting right beside Steve as he wrote the beginning and also the end of the poem.

We used oil pastels for the drawings. They were easy to hold. Using our FC skills, Steve pointed to each color we would use, and I held his hand as lightly as I could to draw, the pastel between his thumb and forefinger. So the colors were his, and drawing was "ours." The other art teacher felt surprised at Steve's vision, how he chose colors: he made the mountains purple, an unusual choice for children who always make mountains blue. I myself see colors poorly.

The big, purple mulberries are memories from our Wisconsin home.

In The Open Land

Letting new thoughts enter,
I find the grassland
looks different.
It is full of thin shapes,
many greens not the same,
sudden colors of flowers
red, purple, yellow, orange.

No hiding from the sun here,
everything wants sunlight,
more light, more heat
is better.

You cannot be afraid on the grassland.
Be bold, be humble.
You are so small, so young.
In the world, you ask
what matters of life?
The grasses answer,
all of us.
Every one.

July 26, 2009

This morning, we left the hotel late and arrived at the grassland after the rest of summer camp in their big bus had departed the first site. We were alone. Steve and I walked out a short way, then sat down so the grasses came to our faces. I was surprised, after Wisconsin prairie, that we could see the ground between the plant stems. Steve grabbed litter, stems to put in his mouth but not too often. We were busy looking.

When we caught up with the group at the second stop, he wanted to join the students who were drawing trees (this landscape was elm savanna). We could sit in the shade, I leaned my back against the small trunk. After he finished drawing, he started this poem.

Nothing Less

Eventually boys must leave the grassland,
we cannot eat grass or flowers.
I look back to landscapes of Keerqin,
they changed me.
They gave me space inside.
The sky has the largest place in my heart,
clouds of white and gray,
when I think of those shapes changing all the time
I find my own feelings mirror heaven . . .
because I am like air,
wind rushes before me.

I do not know where I will settle
far from here and now.
Sometimes I wish I might take root
like the bushes in those mountains.
But I am human,
blessed to move and hope
for nothing less than everything.

July 29, 2009

Steve wrote this poem the evening after we got home. He hadn't had the
chance for poetry during the last two days of our trip. Today we both have
been looking back.

Steve easily feels joy. He accepts his life and yet wants everything. I find
it hard to accept what he has now without feeling afraid I am settling for
less. I do not wish to risk his future by accepting the present. This moment,
however, I understand Steve is risking nothing by his joy, this boy who is
blessed to move.

Waiting and Watching

Grandma sent me a book and a wish.
She wished that I might grow plants
like Stanley Kunitz did.

Back in May, Daddy and I offered a pot,
a home, to two plants.
I thought they would die,
some leaves turned brown,
fell off.
Then we waited and hoped.

Tonight we visited our garden.
It covers the porch in back of the kitchen.
A dozen plants grow here,
some were saved from trash,
even a fern hid in soil we brought from the mountain.
We see one pink flower against the green and dark.

I remember the touch of soil
in my fingers when we began.
Tonight, I go to sleep knowing
the garden watches all night.

August 1, 2009

I suggested we visit the garden only moments before Liying, Steve, and I walked through the kitchen, paused at the door, and then arranged a stool so that Steve and Liying could sit close down by the plants. I stood and read them two Kunitz poems from the book *The Wild Braid*. I suggested that sometime Steve might want to write Grandma about our plants.

After ten minutes with the plants, we went to the bedroom. Steve wanted to write.

He tells me he doesn't know the endings for his poems until he gets to the end. He doesn't skip ahead or realize what the last line will be in advance. I asked him if he ever worried if he could end a poem. *Yes.*

Chance

Good friends can be hard to get.
Tonight we have a chance.
We sit on the bench
while Sasha plays nearby.

But I cannot answer her.
Daddy cannot understand her.
She looks happy,
and she looks our way.

If Mama were here,
I could use FC.
Then Daddy could speak in English
and Mama could translate into Chinese.
But now that can't happen
because Mama cannot be here,
she has a guest for work.

We must sit and wait and watch.

August 4, 2009

On occasional evenings in the courtyard, a Russian girl appears. She is just Steve's age. She pretends not to pay any attention to us, but she plays in our corner of the yard, leaving and returning and half the time smiling or returning my smile. When I held Steve up to grasp the horizontal bars, she pulled up onto the bars and flipped her legs up over the other side, hung there then did it again.

A few evenings earlier, I had Liying tell her (Sasha only speaks Russian and Chinese) to visit us sometime. Five minutes later she rang our doorbell. She and her brother played on Steve's keyboard, Sasha talked to us through Liying.

Tonight I realize, unless something changes, that Steve cannot meet any girls here in Harbin without help from both his father and mother. I mentioned this to our older boy (over the telephone, he is 24 and lives in Chicago), and he said that was very tough.

I never imagined, when I was young, that I would sit waiting and watching with my son.

Sasha didn't know that this would be our last chance, Steve and both his parents and Sasha all together, our last chance until October. It would soon be time for me to leave. But then, what could she have done? It seems that life itself, setting small things aside, is waiting and watching. When the moments come, Steve has told me, *I am ready.*

Between

I want to work hard,
I want to make the world
more beautiful,
a better place for children.

Music

In this life,
we have many choices.
Have we the choice to talk?

If we have that choice,
I will tell everyone
how I felt
when I could only listen,
when my thoughts
were mine alone.

If I never can choose,
still the wren in my heart
will sing,
and I will write my music
in poetry for all to hear.

Dear wren,
that I have you inside
makes me certain
the world is beautiful!

August 31, 2009

Steve wrote this poem after our first, busy day at the Institutes. We sat in such a deep, saggy couch, I knew it would be difficult for me to stand up again with his weight.

The poem made me realize how quickly Steve has moved. It could not be just the 19 days we have been apart. Although the evenings of summer each seem like those before, and Steve has written,

> We pass the days and nights
> as if our time would never end

our time has not stood still. My Steve is hardly the same child who chortled when he received his first gift on February 14.

Steve has always loved music even in the long, early years. We had live music at the Crane Foundation's Christmas party in 2003, and Steve and I sat close by the guitars, together we shook maracas. He learned to whistle that night, we first heard him from the back seat of the car as we drove home.

Driving on the dark country roads, I had been remembering a red glow from a film about volcanoes, fiery lava that crept over the land. That endless fire had underlain my feelings during those years, burning under the busyness of our lives. Steve's whistle felt like cool water.

Stack of Books

Home reminds me
that time passes
and we change.

I see the stack of books
I read a year ago.
Then these books felt so new,
now they feel part of me.
What stack of books
will I find next September?

I hope and work to make
my spirit bigger,
so let's think carefully
about that stack.

September 5, 2009

We arrived from Chicago about supper time, all three of us happy to be
home together in Baraboo. I had left all the books he had read the previous
September in a (tall) stack close by where we placed his bedding on the
living room floor. Since he is a speed reader, the stack was well over a foot
high, a little dusty. But Liying proclaimed the house the cleanest she has
ever seen it (since she moved to China). "Good boy," she said to me.

Hungry

Today we have a chance
for rest and thought.

We stay at home in Baraboo,
we plan our future.
Maybe we can publish a book of poems,
maybe we can write how science
and poetry come together.

All the while out the windows
we see green of plants,
green growing leaves that
reach around us with each hour
more and more hungry

just as we feel hungry
for spirit and hope.
The nature of plants
and humans is the same.
We want light.

September 6, 2009

Steve and I spent much of the day in the living room, where we could
hear Liying in the kitchen (cleaning). I was very aware of the green leaves
outside all the windows, even trying to reach inside through cracks left by
the storm windows. I suggested he write about what he could see outside.
He did not indicate yes or no to this suggestion. Not long after, when he
began the poem, I had no idea the plants had grown into his thought.

Steve loves this home, even though he only comes here once or twice
a year. Wisconsin is close to the same latitude as Heilongjiang and Jilin
so the seasons are the same although here we have burr oaks outside
the window, our prairie oaks, and at Keerqin Mongolian oaks grow. The
kestrels are not quite the same, and winters in Harbin much colder.

Humpty Dumpty

I see how people hurt each other.
In this world, the good that people wish
can hardly repair
the damage that others cause.
If we believe
that life can be beautiful,
we should never stop healing

one hurt then another.
My parents have spent all my life
to put me back together,
they are more than any king's
horses and men.

I can only have the same spirit
to heal what is damaged around me.
Daring to try, I bloom!

September 6, 2009

We went to Devil's Lake State Park, just a ten-minute drive. Steve almost finished reading *A Tree Grows in Brooklyn.* Then he wanted to write a poem. Later he explained that war was starting in the book, that made him want to write.

I have recited Humpty Dumpty almost once a day for weeks and months, whenever I am at our Harbin home while we do patterning with Steve. Steve does not want to lie on the table and tolerate our moving his limbs back and forth unless he has proper entertainment. Fortunately, he is content with listening to my bird song imitations over and over, a few human songs I know, and a little group of nursery rhymes. All of these combined are just enough to occupy the hour we pattern each day. This poem today was the first sign anyone has noticed that we have our own humpty dumpty.

Devil's Lake

Going to Devil's Lake,
we saw the water rippling in the breeze.
We saw colors
from sun and sky
bouncing from those ripples.

Everyone sat facing the moving water
as if the world mirrored their hearts.
I felt it, too,
giving my hopes to the lake.

My thoughts merged with water
and ripples,
became part of something
very big.
Is that freedom?

September 7, 2009

Steve wanted to do this poem before breakfast. He had slept remembering
Devil's Lake from the afternoon before, where we had faced the lake like
everyone else. This park is the most popular in Wisconsin, mostly people
come from Milwaukee and Chicago. The bluffs that rise over the lake are
made of basalt 1.5 billion years old.

Change

In the afternoon,
the sun drops behind the Baraboo Hills,
the water grows dark
except where sky catches on ripples.
One white gull flies back and forth.
We hear children's voices
far over the lake.

I feel autumn comes now.
The nights long and cool,
we linger, listening
watching.
We feel glad
and
a little afraid.
What will happen inside us?
Life doesn't stay the same.

September 7, 2009

Steve and I sat by Devil's Lake. He preferred a bench in the sunlight, but by the time he had finished drinking we sat in shadow of the hills.

The seasons do come into the cities, but spring arrives early and autumn leaves late. In Baraboo, Wisconsin we easily go from home into wild landscapes where the air is quiet. We can feel the change while we sit and wait, it is easier than in Harbin.

Running Day and Night

Nobody else is here,
only you and me and the stream.
We are quiet.
Only the stream speaks.

I wonder how the water
can run day and night
all the hours while we sleep,
all the hours while we join life
with reading and writing and hoping,
all the hours we breathe.

Even while we sit still,
the water whispers,
Never die
never give up
never stop singing
never forget all you have to give.

September 9, 2009

We drove into Baxter's Hollow, parked where we have parked in earlier
years – here is one of the places I fell with Steve — and sat on a point
of grass and stone just above the stream. Almost noon, the forest was
still, hardly any bird sounds, and nothing of people or cars. Almost
immediately, Steve wanted to write.

Popping Smile

Finding how to give,
a serious matter for me
—we must get ideas
for the people around me,
we must think carefully about each one,
we must think carefully about how I can give,
without talking
or walking.

I am so glad that my hands
become stronger and
listening more to my mind.
Soon I can hold gifts in both hands,
maybe even offer them
across the wide air.

Then I will have the popping smile
like the wren in song!

September 9, 2009

Earlier that day, Steve and I went to the International Crane Foundation (ICF), where I work, and we saw his poem *To My Friends* mounted on the wall as part of the exhibit ICF has shown all summer. Meeting ICF staff members, Steve used FC to join our conversations (how much easier than in the courtyard in Harbin!).

During dinner, I read Steve's poem just written a few minutes before (*New Choices*) and told Liying how Steve is now thinking about how he can give to others. These thoughts are such a change for him from simply and always wondering what will happen to him next, not so long ago when he could not make his wishes known . . . the anxiety of having no control.

After dinner, I asked if he wanted to do anything more before sleep. *P o e m*, he spelled on his communication card. He had been thinking.

I had a guess where he got the expression *popping smile*, and asked him. *A Tree Grows in Brooklyn,* he replied and laughed he was so pleased. He had finished the book a few days before. He joined this new expression to his wren theme. He loves to carry images and thoughts from one poem to another. Since it is a Carolina wren, hearing this wren is a highlight of each visit to Philadelphia because they are common there and almost absent from Wisconsin. We have house wrens by our Baraboo home. Winter wrens nest at Baxter's Hollow.

Until the Sun Returns

Stopping by Baxter's Hollow last night
I saw the evening shadows growing
and the night getting ready
to take over the creek.

It is a different creek at night,
all voice, all movement
water hurrying
from dark to dark.
We cannot stay, we only
belong with the light.

I lie in bed at home
I only imagine water and music.
Dark holds us alike
until the sun returns.

September 11, 2009

At Baxter's Hollow a couple days ago, at noon, I had suggested to Steve
that we return when the creek went from day to night, to see what we
might find at that different hour. Yesterday, driving home from Madison, I
diverted us back to Baxter's Hollow. Steve had been afraid before, that we
might fall into the stream. But now he wanted to return to the same spot
by the water.

There was no sun in the valley. We heard a cricket, and a few birds. Like at
noon, a bumblebee fed on asters.

We stayed and kept quiet just a few minutes. We left at 6:40, too early to
see the night arrive. We never mentioned those moments again, but Steve
wanted to write after having his morning water today. Steve let me know, *I
thought this poem this morning in bed.*

His Dream of God

In the place where grassland meets wetland,
the cranes found a snake.
They caught it
despite the wriggles
to escape
and the plants and water that offered hiding,
they lifted it again and again,
dangling from the long beaks.

The snake just got shorter
as we watched
until there was no snake.
In that moment,
I saw death,
that is how life changes
from one creature into another.

I expect that sight many more times
as I grow and watch the wild.
Heaven must wait for snakes
as heaven waits for all of us.

Time will bring us together
like Michelangelo's vision
on the Sistine Chapel wall.
I keep his dream of God before me.

September 10, 2009

We went to the new African exhibit at ICF today, watching the Wattled Cranes with their wetland. Hardly had we sat down, when the cranes found the snake. Liying ran all the way around the exhibit to get pictures of the snake and the crane bills close up.

Steve said he saw the snake. And when Liying returned, he looked with us at the photos on the back of the camera as we blew them up to identify the snake species. Garter snake. But he didn't show any feelings, not even great interest. I was surprised and pleased when later he wrote this poem.

He had never seen a snake, nor predation, one wild creature taking another.

Dreams of Every Boy

Chasing horses did not take long.
They came quickly when Tammy called,
soft, snuffly noses
reached over the gate,
I could feel their breath on my face.

Wide lips opened, teeth
grabbed handfuls of grass and clover.
They peered down at us
through their fly masks,
pushing and eager.

I bellowed, *Yet I want to ride!*
Mama and Daddy hoisted me up.
Chet carried me over just a towel,
high over everyone.
I could look down Chet's long neck
as he reached for grass in Fawn's hand.

All under me I felt his muscles stretch,
his back tilt left
then right, then left again.
He and I felt wind and sunlight,
we could have walked
all the way to Keerqin.

Running over the land and sea,
these dreams carry us to heaven.

September 14, 2009

Steve was eager to write after we visited Tammy and her horses. Since Tammy had no saddle, we had no thought of any riding on horseback for Steve. We would just touch the horses' faces.

Yet Steve's bellow was enough to make things happen quickly. Actually it only felt like a bellow to Steve because of the strength of his feeling. He merely agitated for his FC card and then spelled out what he wanted.

With All My Heart

Tomorrow we leave,
we fly across the ocean
Mama and me,
we will sleep next in China.

Soon I cannot see you.
Soon I cannot share the
thoughts and feelings
that rise when we meet others,
these happy hours that
show me a new life
possible
probable
what I hope will be my future.

We have so much ahead
that will open the world.
Let us plan how to make
more changes when you come to China.
We have much opportunity
whenever we are together.

I will welcome you
with all my heart.

September 14, 2009

This last day went quickly. Steve felt it. I felt it.

How Will I Feel?

We wait.
We see the plane is here.
The door opens and shuts.
Many people are ready to go.
I do not want to leave.

I want to stay
and find out what happens
when night comes to Baxter's Hollow.
Will the insects all sing?
Will an owl catch mice?
Will I feel strong?

I will imagine
as we fly to Beijing.

September 15, 2009

When we arrived at the gate at O'Hare Airport, for the plane Steve
and Liying would take to Beijing (the airline gave me a special pass to
accompany and help Liying with Steve), Steve got suddenly upset. He
remembered a year ago, at the same gate, when the airline staff made it
very difficult for Liying to get Steve plus carry-on luggage onto the plane.

This time Steve was agitated, just as I was, just as Liying was. Aside from
our feelings, the place became more and more crowded. The plane was
late and we waited much longer than expected. When I offered Steve his
FC card, he spelled out *p o e m*. He wrote the first two stanzas, then to my
surprise his finger pointed to *yes* – meaning he was done. Done?

With my prompting, he added two lines.

We had gone to Baxter's Hollow twice, but that was not enough! The
Baraboo Hills are my favorite place – Devil's Lake, Baxter's Hollow, and
other valleys in the hills. I have been coming here for 36 years. Yet it has
been a very long time since I saw the hills with such clarity and feeling as
these explorations with Steve. I feel he has left too soon, we missed the
shadow time.

Autumn

When I eat,
I dream
of running through grassland
and riding horses at Keerqin,
tasting the wind on my tongue

Careless Laughter

Boisterous
we walked among trees
and heard our own laughter.
We joked,
we felt what we said was funny,
so funny that we joked more.

All our noise made the birds hide,
we saw only gulls high in the sky
among clouds piled on top of trees.
No one stopped
when a shrike flew out of leaves
and quickly back into leaves.

I felt happy to walk with friends
and listen to their voices
and know this must be
what life will be like
when I am older and free.

October 4, 2009

Last night, when I asked Steve what he liked best yesterday, he answered *you came home*. Next, he mentioned going outside. *To the city*. Liying said it wasn't to the city. But they DID go outside the gates, the streets there are so noisy on the way to the park. I asked what he liked there. *Gulls.* Liying said they didn't see any gulls, they never walked by the water but stayed up on the dike.

Today Steve didn't seem to have any poetry popping out, so before dinner I suggested he write about that walk the day before with Liying and her students, he could give them the poem. Right after dinner, he wrote.

It is curious how this poem describes what ordinary people miss when they laugh too much: the gulls his mother didn't see, the shrike vanishing into leaves. I asked if he thought life would be better when he is older and free, as he describes at the end, or better now when he sees the gulls and shrike? Or is it mixed? *Mixture,* he answered.

I am reminded of the day Steve wrote about seeing a swallow out the window as we carried him downstairs. But that poem had no ambivalence.

Yesterday Readies Me for Today

Waking to a new day,
I feel eager and curious.
Yesterday surprised me twice.

First, I moved more on pawatee.
Because you touched me,
I became excited and fast!

Second, my poem had feelings
I hadn't recognized —
I now have gifts that others miss because
they talk and run about,
they make too much noise
to see and hear like I do.

Silence helps me find
beauty of the park
like gulls
and mushrooms growing
in the wet of soil and fallen leaves.

Those were yesterday's surprises.
They make me ready
to discover today's.

October 5, 2009

Yesterday when I asked Steve about his poem, he felt surprised when he
looked at what he had just written.

Today I woke very early, and Steve woke earlier than usual. Liying has gone
to a meeting in Japan. Since just the two of us were here, we did not go
straight to drinking water like every other day. Steve wanted to write.

Days With Daddy

When we saw the flowers by the courtyard,
boys ran past,
kicking a ball,
moving so fast
they did not notice the colors
red
and yellow
and purple
and blue
and the orange of nasturtiums
all a blur for them,
but for our eyes
enough to make us happy
for days
for all winter,
and on one red flower,
a black ladybug with orange spots
that opened into wings,
it flew away.

I watched for spiders flying, too,
on silk,
I found them against the blue
not big enough for anyone but me.

Boys laughed and boys shouted,
they bounced as if
nothing mattered but their game.

Daddy and I cared for a different world,
cared for surprise
and spiders in the sky!

October 6, 2009

Yesterday, Steve wrote about nasturtiums, vines growing up bushes by the gate where we walked the short way from courtyard to home. I told Steve how my father loved nasturtiums, and I tried to spell their name for him but couldn't. He spelled the name a different way in the poem. I looked it up on Google, so I could correct the spelling but found he had it right.

Although it is well into October and many blossoms are past, we saw varied flowers in the gardens around the courtyard. I didn't know any names except nasturtium. I asked Steve how he learned that word. He found it in a book, he has forgotten the name but soon I guessed it was about Stanley Kunitz and his gardening. *The Wild Braid*? *Yes.*

Yesterday we sat out on the bench, and I read poetry aloud while he snacked. I found two tiny spiders crawling on the page. They likely had parachuted in, and I told Steve how in autumn the baby spiders disperse by floating in the air, carried by the wind on streamers of their silk. We looked up and around at that moment but did not see any. Steve remembered to look again today. He saw two.

Clouds on Water

Despite all the bickering,
I am happy to have Mama home again.
Her voice makes me calm
because she loves living things
like we do.

All we hope for
can be found simply
in the park by the river.
I remember walking there
and finding a toad with wet skin.
I touched that toad
but Adam said its skin was poisonous,

he helped me wash my hand in the pool
where we let the toad free,
where tiny fish swam away from my fingers,
the clouds lay on the water
while I turned my face toward you
because I felt so happy.

October 8, 2009

It had been a difficult day, yet we had lovely minutes outside in late
afternoon's soft sunlight. Then Steve came inside to pawatee with
renewed energy. At the end of the day, he chose pawatee as his favorite
thing of the day. The same choice as all the other recent days except
yesterday when I didn't ask.

Later I asked if he knew that many people felt clouds were bad, they hurt
the day, our spirits. No, he did not know. He did not have any double
meaning with the title of this poem. Clouds for him are beautiful every day.

The Sun Climbs the Wall

Before we made supper
Daddy took me outside.
We saw the sun on the building.
As we sat, the shadow climbed the wall.

We saw time,
it is always moving,
we are following
but we never catch up.

I wait for moments that stop time,
a dear wren sings,
or the sun goes,
or I find the courage
to try again tomorrow.

October 9, 2009

Because the apartment was noisy from cleaning and cooking for guests coming to dinner, I took Steve outside for his afternoon snack — it is rare he goes outside twice in one day. The day before, at 3:15, we had sat in the warm sun. But at 3:40 today the sun was already too low, and its light did not reach any benches but only the building before us. Before we went in, I pointed out that the sun had moved up the building, up to the sixth floor.

This day wasn't the best. He did poorly on pawatee, and I pushed him some. He didn't like gravity assist but he moved his legs (both of them) more than before. That is something.

112

Both Birds and People

To know both people and birds
I must listen with inner ears.
I cannot be shy,
I cannot make myself too big.

I hope that as the years pass
I will have found
better ways to share myself
with birds and people.

Really it is the same,
the same distance
the same problem of language,
patience.

When this world changes
we will all be one.

October 9, 2009

It was late, past bed time. Steve had already written two poems. Since we
had had fun with the party and he was happy (he indicated his favorite
thing this day was being with people), I asked if he would like to do
anything before sleep. I was surprised he wanted to write.

Voice

During the day I wait for you,
I remember feelings I want to tell you,
I remember little thoughts for you
and begin to put them into
lines and stanzas
that flow like that stream in the hills.

My voice runs day and night
with all my heart,
and when I see you,
my voice turns into words
that anyone can understand.

Don't forget there are many voices
no one ever hears.

October 10, 2009

I was away at crane meetings all day and got home just after 7. Steve was
smiling and eager for FC.

Before Deciding

Before deciding
what to do in the evening
I remember
all the evenings when I had no choice,
all the wishes
I could not tell anyone,
the poems
that vanished into dreams at night.

And I hesitate.
How lucky to choose!
Can I put into words
the feelings
that matter most in this evening,
in this life?

I love the deep music
that runs beneath
that never stops
that is my gift to you,
my sweet song.

When you are away,
I sing to the clouds.
Any cloud
lifts my heart.

October 18, 2009

So often in the evening, when all else is done, Steve and I sit on the bed and I ask him what he would like to do. There are normal choices, but I often say, "Or whatever you want." He has never picked anything out of our routine.

This time, before deciding, he wanted to write. He is right about his gift to me. He often has told me, what is possible is not what we expect. So many times, he has written about change that may happen any time,

> *Later, we will laugh,*
> *we did not know*
> *what would happen, huge.*
> *Later, I will tell my children*
> *that today started my new life*
> *and everything that followed*
> *ever was different.*

Before Supper

Before supper
we have time free for anything.
We even can do nothing!

I can only imagine
how other children would choose.
Study is not for them
caring instead to shout, and run,
devising new ways to laugh.

But I am hungry for more knowing
before supper
after
between bites
any and every time.

I want to know if Raphael
ever watched the sun go
and felt he was losing the world to darkness —
because the colors go
and we are left with feelings
that we can't hide under paint.
Oh, how I wish I could talk to Raphael,
or talk to you tonight.

October 19, 2009

Before supper, we had time. He has been reading a book about Raphael, he could see it on the bed.

I realize he remembers vividly the visit last winter to Liying's cousin in his study, and the painting just started with the brown undercoat. And he remembers well the oil pastels we used to color the mountains, lake, and grasses of Keerqin in July. Maybe he understands painters from the inside.

Elena Smirenski came to dinner, and she brought desert. But when we were done with the main course, since Steve never eats sugar foods, I took him to the bedroom. We sat together and I asked him what he wanted to do. I had our books and papers spread around us. *Eat cake.*

We did.

Circle on the Floor

Many far places come into my mind,
places I would love to see,
but I would rather be here with you
and give our thoughts freedom.

The farthest distance is inside.
It is deciding how deeply I can reach
from heart to muscle
and how much my body can become me.

A flower is a flower
nothing more or less,
spiders even spiders,
days all alike.
But some rare moments only
I am completely
fully
me.

Like when I zoomed down pawatee
and made a circle on the floor.
You felt so amazed!

October 20, 2009

Today was generally good for pawatee. But the last time of all, late in the afternoon, as if someone had lit a fuse, Steve really did zoom down and then onto the flat he kept rocking and pushing, pushing me back and back in a broad circle that shoved me wrong way under the patterning table, and Steve looking back the way he had come – an entire half circle. He felt as surprised as me!

I am happy to remember this moment, but also I remember many high points in months and years past that could not be sustained. For Steve, and for myself, I must find confidence again and again.

When Grasses Speak

Happy people will decide I cannot
think or feel deeply
or that I have nothing to give.
They look away as if I wasn't there
or ask questions
like I couldn't hear.
They miss my life.

At summer camp,
after the children heard my poetry
they started to look into my eyes.

One little boy sang to me
in Mongolian
about the grassland
that I love, too
and both of us remember
a moment when grasses spoke
like I speak now.

小草低语时

幸福的人们认为我不能
不能深沉地思考
不能深切地感受
不能给予
他们总当我不存在
他们提问
却当我听不见
他们错过了我的生命

在夏令营
孩子们听见了我的诗歌
他们开始探寻我的眼睛

一个小男孩对我歌唱
用蒙古语
歌唱草原
我也深爱的草原
我俩都记起
小草低语的那一刻
就像此时我在诉说

October 21, 2009

It is close to a year since Steve wrote his first poem. This morning, I asked him to think about how he has changed in the last year.

This evening after he wrote, I asked if he was responding to my suggestion. *Yes.* Yet something quite unexpected came out. I feel lucky. We had never talked about the boy at Keerqin. That hot afternoon when we had all gathered in the yurt, I read aloud Steve's poems in English for the children. And Liying spoke them in Chinese. The boy walked right up to us, where we sat in the yurt, he knelt and sang.

I asked Steve when he composed this poem. He replied, *When we went outside and boys came and stared.* This afternoon as we sat on the bench outside, two boys had been wildly skateboarding; they walked up and did stare, and said things in Chinese that sounded unpleasant. When Steve first wrote the poem, he began the first line with *bad* but later changed to *happy.*

I often send Steve's poems to friends. This poem went to a Chinese friend who had attended summer camp. She in turn shared it with a friend who translated it and asked if she could put Steve's poem into her blog. Steve was pleased.

Just Like Me

Going outside in days with wind,
even catching the sunlight
I feel winter.
I see boys in coats
running to keep warm
and see women in bigger coats
not warm.

The red flowers fade.
Only the nasturtium is bright,
leaves perfect,
just like the October long ago
when Daddy's father died.
The nasturtiums bring me close to him.

I never knew or heard his laugh
but I guess he liked
flowers, birds, forests, mountains
just like me
maybe we would have read
together like Daddy and me.

Maybe someday a boy I never know
will like poetry
just like me.

October 24, 2009

Late October, and the flowers are still fading along the edges of the courtyard. Low to the ground, sheltered by the taller plants but looking out are several nasturtiums, still untouched by winter. I have told Steve they remind me of my father. And because I am reminded, I have been telling Steve about Dad, how he liked to joke and he laughed more than anyone else at his own jokes, how he took on bigger gardens and more projects than he could ever complete, how I found his nasturtiums when I drove down so suddenly to the farm, arriving early on October 17, the morning after he died.

When the Swallows Return

For us,
today gave the chance
to see the river at year's end.

The sky cloudy and light dim,
the swallows made silhouettes right above the treetops,
right above the last leaves,
a few still green
but most yellow and falling.

We touched the poplars,
smooth and gray,
and heard the tut-tuts of bramblings
so different than in spring.

A day I will remember all winter,
and I will look back happily
that we had the chance to walk by the river
spring and fall.
But I too have changed,

I know now my thoughts will not blow away like the leaves.
They are like the swallows,
flying away and returning after winter
more alive than ever.

Before then, I will tell you, dear Daddy,
what I hope to find:
a better way to hear
even the wings of a dream.

October 25, 2009

I was excited looking ahead to our outing today, especially after the delightful weather yesterday. Today unfortunately had clouds. We bundled Steve up. He looked cold and not too expressive. Often his head is tilted down, slightly to one side or another, and he tends to chew his coat, which also brings his head down. But I realize he is looking, at the times he wants to look. He looked at the white rumps of the brambling flying away.

His looking is quicker than ours, as if he is sure with a brief glance, not needing time to be certain. For years after his injury, he could not look at anything directly – vision was so intense it hurt.

Thinking about the end of his poem, I remember that hearing also is different for him than for us, it is hard to imagine him hearing better except to catch voices that we haven't known.

I nearly forgot the most amazing part of the walk. There were four or five swallows, one came close enough I knew it was a barn swallow. I have never seen swallows so late in October in Wisconsin, and would have guessed they would long be gone. As if Steve's swallow poems had held them here.

Yellow of Poplars

Bodies tell us who we are
and bodies are all
that other people see.
Yet are legs and arms us,
or am I the soul that lives inside?

I feel as much as anyone
but I cannot feel with my left hand
or my deep muscles don't respond.
Other people only notice the outside
or they don't look at all.

My wish is to break out,
for the inner me to shine
like yellow of poplars
or the summer flowers,
red that hasn't faded.

I think that is why I like birds,
because their voices
soar far above.

October 26, 2009

Steve wrote before dinner. Just like in Wisconsin in late October, the
brightest color along the river were poplars still bright yellow and leafy.
Yellow leaves against the gray trunks. I like how much Steve takes in what
we see on our walks. He is insatiable.

Believe in Better Days

Believe the future
will be different than the past,
I am confident that is a better way to live.

Yesterday I worried that my progress would
never change, that I would never
crawl or creep or walk
but live like a tree that had restless roots
or like a flower that only moved
when no one was looking.

Today I realized I am more
like the swallow that doesn't
have legs so it flies.

Fortunately it is not too late to tell you
that I might be in the Philippines tomorrow!
I treasure each day whoever I am.

October 27, 2009

Steve and I have not slept well in recent nights. We were tired all day, and
pawatee was muted for us both. This poem surprised me tonight, so light
on a tired day. And finally we see the title poem to his first e-book of poetry
that he named, *Believe a Better Day Will Come*. We made this ebook after
his first season of poetry, in February.

Yet all this time, he has been saving that title for the right poem.

Listen

Any fear
can hold us back from our dreams.
Today I felt afraid
that I could not crawl.
I felt my legs heavy
my arms stuck
my hips frozen like ice,
I just went still.

Then I heard a voice,
was it my voice,
or someone beside us?
I didn't know
that listening was the way to crawling.

Courage, we seemed to say.
You can move
whether the feeling is there
or not.
And so I did.

October 29, 2009

I have noticed some small signs of change with pawatee. As Steve wrote a couple days ago, can these moments last?

Coming onto the flat, he seems to run out of steam, and then – with my encouragement – he gets going again. Before, once he started moving, he had to keep going. Now, it seems he can push the "on" switch when he wishes. We will see.

Remembering that he wrote, after reading Mary Oliver's *Poetry Handbook,* that he wanted to revise his poems more, I read him a series of September poems from Wisconsin and asked if he wanted to revise *Humpty Dumpty* or *Gift of the Sun.* In both cases, he pointed immediately to just the lines that gave me problem. He revised both.

Four Seasons

A time for change is here.
Every morning we go outside,
more plants have turned brown,
the flowers shriveling and dead.

All around, life is less, simpler
even the people hide indoors
or hurry through the courtyard.
Daddy shows me nasturtiums
hiding beneath taller plants.
Every day we say goodbye.

But I am glad for winter and a new world.
We start again,
and we will find another four seasons
as beautiful as we remember
and we too will be just the same
and different,
we can hardly imagine how,

counting blessings
that grow with time and wisdom,
even foolish as we will always feel
as if we never saw a flower
open in spring,
or heard a katydid sing on summer nights.
And soon swallows will be leaving again
like last week over the tree tops.

You and I will be waiting
just like now,
and look at each other.
We both will smile.

October 30, 2009

I must admit I have been prompting Steve to write about the seasons, much as I have suggested other topics for his poetry. Destruction has surrounded us these recent days, every day we find less surviving in the bits of garden around the courtyard. It is hard to imagine we saw one of those two-spotted ladybugs just days ago, or that a butterfly flew into the house and among us as we patterned yesterday.

The last days have been difficult, both of us lacking sleep night after night because of that breathing machine. Usually at the end of the afternoon, he is eager and happy at the free hours. This time, after he wrote to my friend Azin, I asked him what he wanted to do. His response was *eat*. We did.

I don't know where he found the serenity to write this poem. He told me he composed it right after lunch, while he lay in the breathing machine, thus shortly after we had gone out and witnessed the latest ravages of frost. I was so tired I worried I had mistaken parts of his poem. And he said yes, I had mistaken a few words and he had already fixed them. That happened when he was revising, he changed three places.

Enough for All of Us

Days pass strangely fast
and I wish to slow them down.
I want more time to feel,
to think,
to know
what is changing in me.

I am realizing
I am becoming
full of gifts for everyone
for anyone:
the woman whose husband lives in prison,
the woman whose body hurts,
the woman whose heart is bad,
my parents who work so hard for me.

Life is not easy for us,
and yet I have joy,
enough for all of us!

November 2, 2009

I am just back from a day and a half in Beijing. I was curious if he would write a conversational poem, like he usually does when I am returning. Not this time.

In the afternoon, I told Liying and Steve about the woman who had translated his poem into Chinese, how her husband was in prison. Liying also told me, so Steve heard too, that Geng who has taken care of Steve for more than four years now must stop because she has a heart problem. And I told Steve that he had another warm message from Azin in Tehran.

Before supper, he had two poems to write. He has never offered two at once. I thought he was just hesitant about which one to write first. He chose this one, and wrote it more slowly, with more interruptions than usual. He didn't look especially joyful, but quite serious. This life is serious.

Can I Keep Them?

Any moment it can happen,
any moment I can feel delight
at a beautiful memory.

Now winter is back,
living is remembering
people, places, movement
all deepening
like nothing became
complete before I had time to feel.
Can I keep these memories until they are ready?

Beneath my days,
memories live,
my heart hears them.
I believe I must put them into words.

Healing is what I can give.
Healing is my calling.

November 2, 2009

This, the second poem, came after dinner, and took more than an hour to write. We could do almost nothing else before bedtime. He would stop and rub his forefinger against his other hand. I must admit I got impatient, and finally angry (!). He had the poem all his head, I think he was struggling with putting it out via FC, whether it was sharing the words with me or having me write them down, somehow these actions made the poem in his head more real, irrevocable. Steve is deeply considering what his life is about.

I kept as patient as I could, and finally put his left hand out of reach of his right, and then he went faster. I felt so tired and pressured today, what kept me with him for this slow emergence was that I could not bear to shut off his communication, or make his thoughts stay inside for another day, or maybe forever.

He is right. So often I have felt calmed and comforted sitting by Steve.

Borrowing from the Past

Another evening with you,
before sleep we depend on this hour
to learn, to write,
to labor for what matters most,
the spirit within our lives.
Any hopes we have rise now
like flowers in spring.

We carry all the seasons
always inside,
we reach back,
the memories are rich.

We put them together in new ways
that show us what has happened.
This is about healing.

November 3, 2009

This poem followed right along from the ones yesterday, all part of the same searching within. He wrote more quickly, but again he started rubbing his right forefinger against his left hand. In months past, when he got to something difficult for him to share (as if he felt unsure of my reaction), he would look at me rather than the communication card, and rub his face against mine.

When I put his left hand aside, again he went more quickly.

After he had finished, and we had read the poem aloud three times without any corrections (I didn't see any either), I suggested for tomorrow he write about some of those memories that rise like flowers. We will see what he does.

By this Time

By this time of day
I have thought for hours
about what I must write.
I have remembered
conversations long ago
about my future

that looked all sadness and hardship.
At our home,
we could not hope
for my mind or body,
many nights we went to bed
without hope.

But inside, I knew hope
that I could return.
But I could not tell you,
I could not comfort you.
You believed I was gone.
I felt joy,
and you felt such sadness.

Just how long have I waited
to tell you I am fine.
I am all alive!
One day we will look back on tonight
and wish we could have known our future.

November 4, 2009

Last night Steve wrote about memories in general, and I suggested that next he express some of those memories that rise inside.

He had thought hard about what he wished to write. After he finished the poem, I talked and he replied by FC. Do you know where your hope comes from? *No*. From your mother? *Some*. From inside or outside? *Inside*. When you wrote *comfort you*, who is "you"? *Daddy*. What about Mama? *She did not need comfort.*

I have long depended on Steve. We depend on each other. Every day I am bringing him what astonished Miranda called, from her lonely island, "O brave new world!"

Kestrel Above

Each moment
I depend on imagination
to keep myself believing

that I will find life expanding
far beyond what I have known.
This November is so different
from last.
Why should I not plan
for more change?

Listening to the kestrel
out the window,
I see the world as he does
the world small below my wings
and moving fast,
the people hardly noticing
the sky that is full and deep.

November 5, 2009

Steve was on the patterning table, the four of us standing around him and
about to begin. Someone had left the window open. I heard short, shrill
calls. I hurried to the window, looking up and around. The kestrel flew over
the top of the next apartment building and out of sight.

Immediately I asked Steve if he had heard it. *Yes.* No one else had. Had he
seen it? *No.* I showed him and the others the picture of the kestrel in our
bird book, its wings pointed for swift flight.

Steve lives partly in a different world. My hand, pulled by his, has brought
me deeper into that other place. Other times, I feel I am calling him – as
Liying and I called while he lay in coma – not to the life he has missed
during the darkness but somewhere brighter, musical.

140

Deep Days

Going outside in snow
feels like we've gone farther
than on other days,
the sky looks closer
with little pieces

falling and hitting our faces,
ready to freeze us
if we don't move all the time.
We do move,
snow is exciting!

On your hair, white gathers.
Since we couldn't go up
to the clouds today,
the clouds came down.

Life can be just that way.
I open mouth and eyes,
no matter that I cannot run,
beauty blows over me,
melts on my tongue.

November 14, 2009

When I returned last night from Beijing, a strong snowfall in Harbin made the drive home slow. I was eager to see Steve before he slept. I looked in the room. I saw almost a man lying on his back on the bed, I didn't recognize him for a moment. He was so big.

Today it snowed lightly, and we could see children and parents playing in the courtyard. Steve was very eager to go out, which we did at twilight when his program was mostly done.

I checked back on Steve's first poem. He wrote just one poem in 2008, on November 23. I continued reading the early poems. Clearly it is Steve then and now, but I am surprised how his voice has deepened. I realize I have changed as well, I see more everywhere I look — as if I too could remember not seeing — and I realize how much I count on Steve for healing.

More Owls

Behind our home is a lumber yard.
Nothing happens there,
no people go inside
as if the place was empty.
We always hurry to the other side
of home, the courtyard
where the children played
in snow the last two days.
We went too, at twilight

when we had to look in the car lights
to see thin snow falling
or feel its whisper on our skin.
At last we turned back
walking toward our door.
Out from the lumber yard

flew the owl seeking mice
it had round wings and round head
and no sound of feathers.
It circled
swooped
and disappeared!
Darkness is hardly the time

to meet new life.
I will remember the owl
in the days ahead
because I saw it with Daddy
our last evening.
Owl reminds me that joy
comes suddenly

. . . even when we don't see Daddy.
I believe that more owls are coming
at the sad times
just like now.

November 15, 2009

This poem took 40 minutes to write, because it is long and because he wrote just before I would leave for America. Over two months apart. He looked very sad by the end. As usual, we sat with him right in front of me, so he could lean against me and keep his balance. At that ending, I just put my arms around him, and we gently rocked.

The story Steve wrote is just how it happened. I saw the owl three times in a few moments, and so did Steve. I think he noticed it before I did. Guo, who walked with us, did not see the owl at all. A memorable first owl, medium sized, probably the long-eared owl.

Our year too is ended. That November evening, 12 months ago, I did not want to lose sleep because Steve loved writing music, so I substituted writing a poem. I could not imagine where that whim would take us. The surprise is just what Steve has written so much about, amazement that more than what we dream is real.

We do not know what lies ahead. Mobility and friendship, love and children? Or something else?

I worry for him. I know there are bitter times waiting. Yet, *I believe that more owls are coming.*

For all of us. Steve has joy enough. If I too choose joy, we will find more than owls: flocks of wrens, nasturtiums flowering, almost always we will breathe the stream's song.

A month earlier, on October 21, I had asked him to write about what had changed over the last year. The next day, I asked him to look ahead.

What the Swallow Sees

Going into the future
I realize that life doesn't stay the same.
We cannot know
how chance will surprise us,
we cannot control,
we cannot decide.

We look inside
for a sense
for where our heart takes us,
much eagerness
to touch others' hearts
to share what deepens each of us,

catch the last light of the sun.
Like the tops of the buildings last night,
like the tops of the clouds out my window
like the swallows
that can fly as far as I can imagine.

Compared to our short view,
the swallows' horizon
vanishes where the earth curves away.
Somewhere past that curve
waits our future.
Caring will guide us.

October 22, 2009

Notes

Quotations on section pages come from other poems by Steve.

Page 33 (Winter): Steve wrote *One Day* on January 29, 2009.

Page 49 (Spring): He wrote *Only You* on May 2, 2009.

Page 65 (Summer): *More Evenings Like This One* was written on July 30, 2009.

Page 85 (Between): *I Can Give* was written at the Institutes on September 2, 2009 as a thank you to the staff members who worked with him.

Page 105 (Autumn): *Farther Than Mountains* was written on July 21, 2009, shortly before we went to summer camp at Keerqin.

Other quotations

Page 87: In the commentary on *Music,* I quote from *Dropping Beautiful Flowers,* written on May 4, 2009.

Page 116: In the commentary on *Before Deciding*, I quote from Steve's poem *Ever Different,* written on September 2, 2009.

www.ingramcontent.com/pod-product-compliance
Lightning Source LLC
Chambersburg PA
CBHW081231090426

42738CB00016B/3253